DADDY, AM I LOVED?

Author by Ulysa Mashell

Once upon a time there was a little girl.
She had brown curly hair she loved to twirl.

She asked her father daddy am I loved? Her face filled with a frown. He answered of course my dear! Come here, sit down.

Her father smiled, as he gazed into her eyes,
He explained there are many ways to love,
but this way I will try.

Look at the flowers in the garden here,
each pedal is proof that love is near.
Love is patient, love is kind.
You can see it with every petal on that vine.

The vine is a stem that
holds them up.
Lovingly feeding them and
filling their cup.

See the birds singing in the tree.
Their loving Melody puts
you at ease.

The little girl looked all around with big wide eyes.
She saw love in the sky, floating about in butterflies.

She felt it in the warmth of the sun.
Inside she knew recognizing love had just begun.

She remembered all the times her father patiently listened. Understanding now his love, she was never missing.

Even when her stories were long.
Her father's love was strong.

Even in the smallest things the girl
saw love and the joy it brings.
Like the way her cat would cuddle
her and chase a ball of string.

Or the way, her dog without fail.
When she came around,
would wag his tail.

Her father held her tight while whispering really low.
You are loved by me more than you will ever know.

The little girl smiled her heart at ease.
Convinced that she was loved, feeling very pleased.

The little girl grew up and ventured out.
Knowing she was loved without a doubt.

She carried love with her wherever she roamed.
Knowing she was loved meant to her, she was never alone.

She spread love wherever she went.
Believing love had to have been God sent.

Love is all around if you just take a look. You should definitely know you are loved after reading this book.

THE END

Made in the USA
Columbia, SC
01 July 2023